# Poems About Me

| | |
|---|---|
| Ten Little Fingers | 2 |
| I Wiggle My Fingers | 6 |
| My Hands | 8 |
| My House | 12 |
| My Puppy | 14 |
| Look at Me! | 16 |

# Ten Little Fingers

I have ten little fingers,
    And ten little toes,
Two little arms,
    And one little nose.

One little mouth,

    And two little ears,

Two little eyes,

    For smiles and tears.

One little head,

    And two little feet,

That dance up and down,

    As I move to the beat.

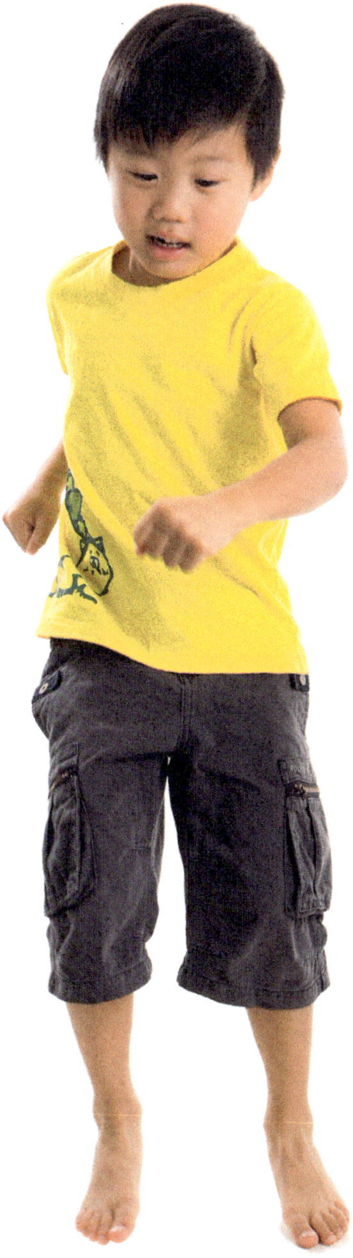

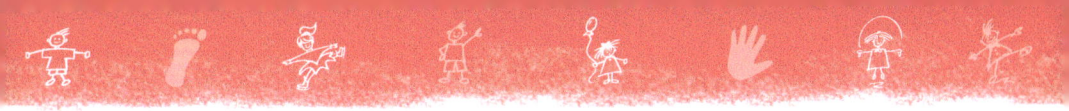

# I Wiggle My Fingers

I wiggle my fingers.

I wiggle my nose.

I wiggle my shoulders.

I wiggle my toes.

Now no more wiggles

Are left in me,

So I'm as quiet ...

    as quiet can be!

# My Hands

My hands upon my head
 I'll place,

Upon my shoulders,
 On my face,

At my waist,

And by my side,

And then behind me

They will hide.

Then I'll raise them
 Way up high,

And let my fingers
 Fly... fly... fly!

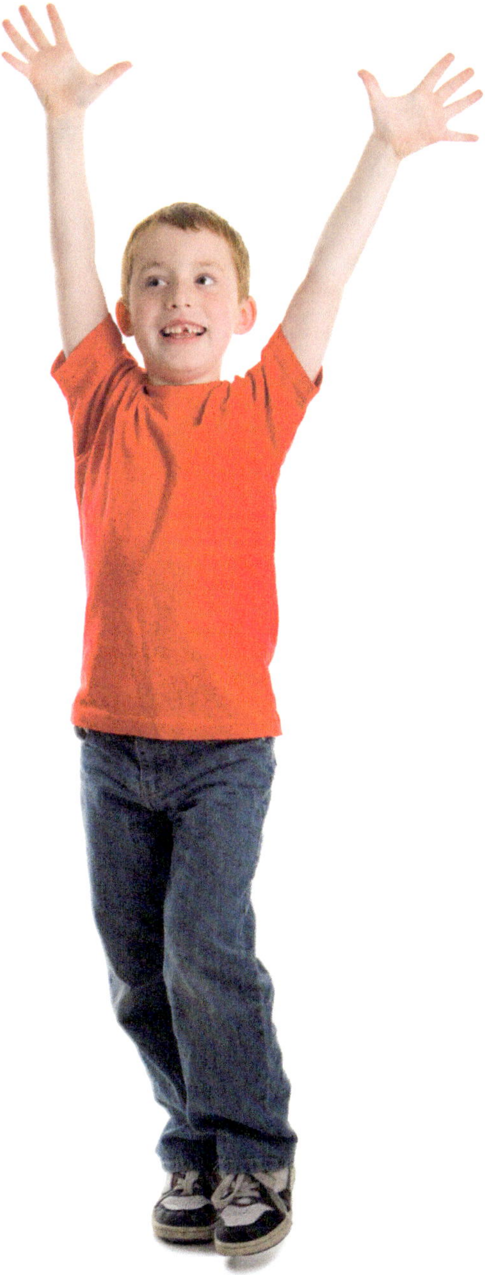

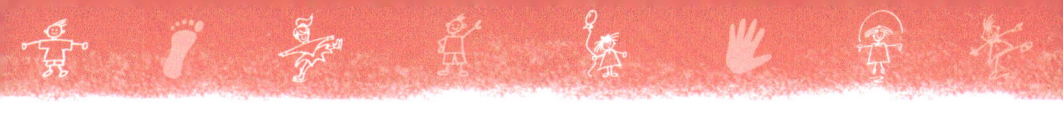

# My House

Here is my house

With a chimney tall.

Here is the tree

That hangs over the wall.

Here are the windows,
Open wide.

And here are my friends,
Playing inside.

# My Puppy

I have a little puppy.

His name is Tiny Tim.

I put him in the bathtub

To see if he could swim.

He drank up all the water.

He ate up all the soap.

And now my puppy's sick in bed,

With bubbles in his throat!

# Look at Me!

I can stand up
    Big and tall.
I can roll up
    Very small.

I can stretch up
    Really high.
And touch the clouds
    Floating by.